Dr Kerry Boyle is a singing teacher, choral director, researcher, arranger and author. As a singing teacher, she has worked with individuals and groups of every age and ability in schools, colleges, universities, extra-curricular music centres and a range of community settings. As a vocal coach and choral director, she has also worked with adult choirs, youth choirs, children's choirs, theatre companies and chamber ensembles. Kerry currently combines her work as a singing teacher, lecturer and associate researcher at Canterbury Christ Church University with tuition and choral direction in various institutional and community settings.

Yasmine Khamellah is a specialist Speech and Language Therapist with a focus on voice, swallowing and communication challenges. She supports individuals navigating singing, communication or swallowing difficulties with warmth, creativity and compassion. Yasmine is recognised for her person-centred approach, creating a safe and collaborative environment for meaningful change. Drawing on knowledge from music, psychology and computer science, she delivers integrated care tailored to everyone. Yasmine's clinical expertise empowers individuals to regain confidence in their voice, communication and swallowing.

Kerry Boyle and
Yasmine Khamellah

A Practical Handbook for Singers

With guidance, tips
and exercises
for healthy singing

AUSTIN MACAULEY PUBLISHERS®
LONDON * CAMBRIDGE * NEW YORK * SHARJAH

Copyright © Kerry Boyle and Yasmine Khamellah 2025

The right of Kerry Boyle and Yasmine Khamellah to be identified as authors of this work has been asserted by them in accordance with sections 77 and 78 of the Copyright, Designs and Patents Act 1988.

All rights reserved. No part of this publication may be reproduced, stored in a retrieval system or transmitted in any form or by any means, electronic, mechanical, photocopying, recording or otherwise, without the prior permission of the publishers.

Any person who commits any unauthorised act in relation to this publication may be liable to criminal prosecution and civil claims for damages.

The story, experiences, and words are the author's alone.

A CIP catalogue record for this title is available from the British Library.

ISBN 9781035891177 (Paperback)
ISBN 9781035891184 (ePub e-book)

www.austinmacauley.com

First Published 2025
Austin Macauley Publishers Ltd®
1 Canada Square
Canary Wharf
London
E14 5AA

We would like to thank all of the students, teachers, performers and practitioners who have inspired and informed this book.

Table of Contents

Introduction — 9

Part One — 11

The Voice — 11

How Does the Voice Work? — 12

    Posture and sound production — 15

    The Pharynx — 22

    The Nasal Cavity — 24

    The Oral cavity — 24

    Jaw — 24

    Lips — 25

    Tongue — 25

    The Hard and Soft Palate — 27

Singing And the Brain — 27

Vocal Health — 29

Some Do's and Don'ts — 36

How to Practice Effectively — 41

Getting Ready For a Performance	**65**
Part 2 Practical Exercises for Singers	**67**
Posture	**68**
Breathing Exercises	**70**
Vocal Exercises	**73**
1. Even Tone	*77*
2. Arpeggio exercise	*79*
3. Descending thirds with short breath	*81*
4. Intervals	*82*
5. Ascending and descending thirds	*83*
6. Introduction to Staccato	*84*
7. Extended Staccato arpeggios	*85*
8. Skipping	*86*
9. More Extended arpeggios	*87*
10. Hysterical Owl	*88*
11. Ways into running	*89*
References	**90**

Introduction

This book is a collaboration between a professional singing teacher and a highly specialist speech and language therapist and provides informed advice on the physical aspects of voice production, including vocal health, along with a range of useful exercises to develop breath control and strengthen tone. The material is presented in two sections, the first providing information and guidance and the second featuring a selection of practical exercises. The book is suitable for singing students and anyone who aims to improve their understanding of voice use and develop safe, effective strategies to improve and enjoy their own instrument.

We believe in celebrating each individual voice and encouraging individuals to develop an understanding of how healthy singing should both *feel* and *sound* so that they are able to practice and perform independently. Aspects of vocal technique can be shrouded in mystery and are often communicated in a highly individual way by teachers through imagery and analogy or tactile cues (touch). While imagery and analogy can be useful in communicating features of musical interpretation it is also important to encourage an understanding of how effective breath control or technique should *feel* for the individual. Furthermore, a reliance on tactile approaches can result in students being uncomfortable in lessons and unable to practice effectively without the support of the teacher.

This book provides useful information and guidance on aspects of posture, breath control and tone production and includes a range of useful tips, tools and exercises to help support safe, sustainable and fulfilling voice use. The exercises are tried and tested with singers of every age and ability and can help to develop and enhance stamina, control and tone quality, thereby improving confidence. These exercises can also be used with individuals or groups, either in isolation to improve and develop specific technical aspects of singing or in combination as part of a regular warm-up sequence.

Part One

The Voice

Voice is a multidimensional concept. In music, the voice is an instrument to express thoughts and feelings and manipulated for artistry effect. It's the most personal and versatile musical instrument, unique to everyone. Physiologically, its viewed as a complex system involving the brain, the respiratory system, larynx, vocal cords, and articulators to enable communication and maintain homeostasis. Psychologically, voice reflects and influences emotional states, identity, and self-concept. It enables us to connect to others. Lastly, at a spiritual stance, voice is viewed as a mode for spiritual energy and connection such as, healing, meditation and chanting. These dimensions of voice can be interconnected. For example, singing is connected to artistry which is impacted by manipulation and control of the physiological system.

An important part of achieving success as a singer involves getting to know the strengths and weaknesses in our voice and finding ways to develop technically so that we can feel confident that we are using our instrument properly and effectively. In this first section, we explore the physiology of the voice and the way in which vocal sound is created.

How Does the Voice Work?

Making a musical sound requires a generator (air from the lungs), a vibrator (vocal folds, in the larynx) and a resonator (the articulators; tongue, soft palate, lips) (Figure 1). The generator causes movement; that movement, in turn, causes the vibrator to vibrate. The resonator enhances vibrancy and sound and creates words. The musculature relevant to singing includes the intercostal muscles, diaphragm, pelvic floor muscles (pelvic diaphragm), lumbar muscles, laryngeal muscles and neck muscles.

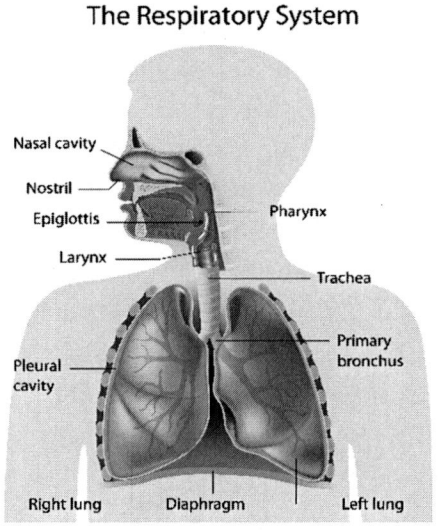

Figure 1: Generator, vibrator, resonator system

In singing, the generator is the breath as voice is generated by air from the lungs. The main structures that help generate breathing and breath control in singing include the lungs, intercostal muscles, diaphragm and pelvic floor muscles (pelvic diaphragm). The pelvic floor diaphragm looks similar in shape to the diaphragm. In our daily lives, we tend to use only a small proportion of our lung capacity. As we explore breathing techniques for singing, we can enhance and develop existing breath control and this, can have a positive impact on other aspects of life.

Through the inhale phase of singing, air quickly enters the lungs, filling the alveoli sacs. This is also achieved with the help of the diaphragm. The diaphragm is a dome shaped muscle. It is shaped like this to accommodate the liver and stomach. The liver and stomach are located just below the diaphragm.

During inhalation, the diaphragm contracts and flattens. This downward movement increases the thoracic cavity's volume, thus drawing air into the lungs. Since the diaphragm is connected to the lungs, the diaphragm's downward movement also pulls the lungs downward, allowing them to expand. At the same time, the abdominal organs, including the liver and intestines, are displaced, causing the abdomen to push outward. This results in the belly bulging slightly as the lungs fill with air (Figure 2).

The breathing out phase in singing (exhalation) is crucial, as this facilitates sound production. During exhalation, the diaphragm relaxes and moves upward. This upward movement happens as the diaphragm releases its contraction and returns to its resting dome shape.

A lot of emphasis is placed on having a "relaxed abdomen," but relaxing the abdomen doesn't mean relaxing everything. The abdomen consists of four layers of muscles (transversus abdominis, rectus abdominis, external obliques, and internal obliques). These muscles need to be engaged appropriately to aid in exhalation. When exhaling, intra-abdominal pressure increases, which pushes the diaphragm upward, closing the thoracic cavity and helping to squeeze air out of the lungs with effective pressure and force. Proper engagement is achieved through correct posture, which is discussed later in this book.

Overall, additional muscle activity and force are not required during the inhalation and exhalation phases in singing, and attempting to use them can be dangerous, as it may lead to laryngeal and neck muscle tension.

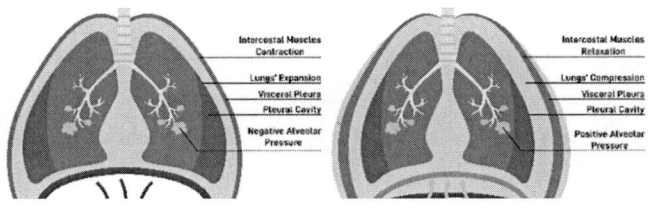

Figure 2: Diaphgram movment during inilation and exhilation

Often, there is a desire to suck in the tummy for aesthetic reasons, which causes tension in the abdominal wall. As a singer, if the waist is sucked in, the abdominal muscles are contracted, restricting the outward expansion of the abdominal cavity during breathing. This restriction creates resistance during the descent phase of the diaphragm as it contracts and fills the lungs with air. As a result, the individual may run out of breath due to insufficient air intake. Singing without enough air also leads to increased tension in the neck and larynx. Therefore, it is crucial for singers to understand

and relax the abdominal muscles, allowing sufficient space for the passage of air and reducing unnecessary tension.

Posture and sound production

Although the abdomen should remain relaxed, singers must ensure that the rest of the body stays engaged and that proper posture is maintained. The pelvic muscles should be engaged to support good posture. This can be achieved by keeping the pelvis in a neutral position. Anatomically, women tend to have a natural forward pelvic tilt compared to men. Standing in a hyper-arched position (Figure 3) can compromise the exhalation process, as the lower back muscles are more likely to be locked in an extended position. In this posture, when attempting to contract the abdominal muscles during exhalation, a dead-end point has occurred because the back and abdominal muscles cannot contract simultaneously.

To reduce this tilt, engaging the gluteus muscles (the bum muscles) can help. By contracting the pelvic muscles, the abdominal area can remain relaxed. To assess whether the pelvic floor muscles are engaged correctly, one can try wearing a horizontal belt or focus on the waistline.

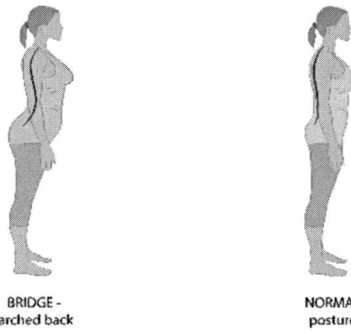

Figure 3: Posture

Common posture mistakes to watch out for:

- ***Overcorrecting the spine:*** Making the back too rigid and straight can be just as harmful as poor posture.
- ***Slumping***: Allowing the spine to slump exaggerates the natural curves in the neck and lower back, which can lead to discomfort.
- ***Knee locking:*** Standing with locked knees and braced thigh muscles pushes the knees backward.
- ***Leaning on one leg:*** Putting all or most of the weight on one leg causes one hip to jut out, creating an imbalance in the pelvic area.
- ***Poor weight distribution:*** Leaning too far forward or backward, improper weight distribution can throw spinal alignment off.

- ***Over-contracting the upper back:*** Pulling shoulder blades too far back narrows the back and disrupts natural posture.
- ***Sunken ribcage:*** This can cause shoulders to round forward, affecting overall posture.
- ***High, tense shoulders:*** Holding shoulders too high and tight encourages shallow breathing from the upper chest.
- ***Tensing the neck:*** Over-constricting neck muscles can force the head backward and push the chin up, which causes neck strain.
- ***Incorrect eye level:*** If eye level is too high or low, it can cause neck tension

How to encourage good posture:

- ***Balance weight:*** Make sure the weight is evenly distributed, with feet about hip-width apart.
- ***Relax legs:*** Keep legs relaxed to avoid knee locking or tensing the thighs.
- ***Align pelvis:*** Keep the pelvis balanced and level—not too far forward or backward.
- ***Lift the ribcage:*** Relax and lift the ribcage to create a sense of space between the lower ribs and hips, giving a more open, free-feeling midsection.
- ***Expand the back:*** Focus on creating space between the shoulder blades to give the back a broad, open feeling.
- ***Relax shoulders:*** Let the shoulders drop and relax, which will reduce tension in the upper chest. Keep

them in a neutral position to avoid pulling them too far back.
- ***Let arms hang naturally:*** Allow arms to hang loosely from the shoulders, keeping hands and fingers free from tension.
- ***Free the neck:*** Lengthen the back of the neck and relax the front, keeping tension away from the shoulders.
- ***Balance the head:*** Keep the head in a neutral, balanced position so it can move easily and effortlessly.

During the exhalation phase of singing, an optimal posture that involves gluteus activation (engaging the glute muscles) and maintaining a neutral pelvis can help achieve a relaxed abdomen and proper activation of the abdominal musculature. This action is dependent on maintaining good posture and allowing the lower back to relax.

Adjusting to a new posture may feel unfamiliar or uncomfortable at first. This is because muscles need time to adapt to the new alignment, especially if specific habits have been developed over many years. With consistent practice, the body will gradually adapt, and the new posture will begin to feel more natural.

During singing, various anatomical structures work in coordination to generate and regulate airflow, which then passes through the true vocal folds. The true vocal folds, located within the larynx, are the primary structures responsible for sound production. There is one pair of true vocal folds and one pair of false vocal folds. The true vocal folds vibrate as the exhaled air passes through them, creating sound waves that result in the voice. The space between the vocal folds is called the glottis.

In singing, it is very important to avoid excessive use of the false vocal folds, as their engagement can lead to muscle tension dysphonia (also referred to as muscle tension voice disorder). The length of the true vocal folds typically ranges from approximately 12.5 mm to 23 mm, with variations based on factors such as gender, age, and body size.

When singing, laryngeal movement is influenced by the coordinated action of various structures within the larynx. The larynx itself is composed of cartilages, ligaments, muscles, membranes, and mucosal lining, all of which contribute to its function in voice production (Figure 4).

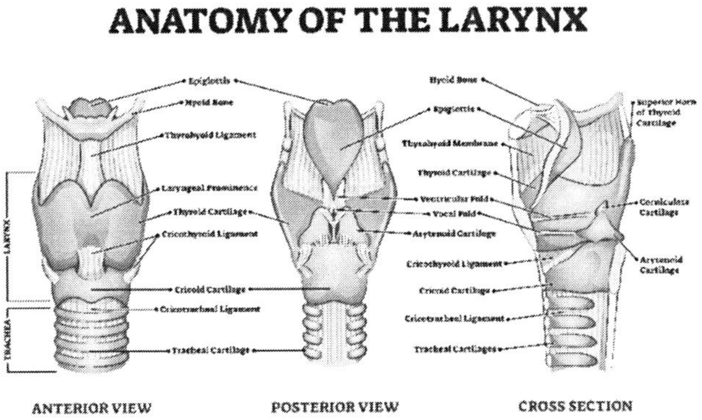

ANATOMY OF THE LARYNX

Figure 4: Anatomy of the larynx

The larynx consists of nine cartilages and one bone (the hyoid bone). Three of these cartilages are paired: the arytenoid, corniculate, and cuneiform cartilages. The remaining cartilages are unpaired: the thyroid, epiglottis, and cricoid cartilages.

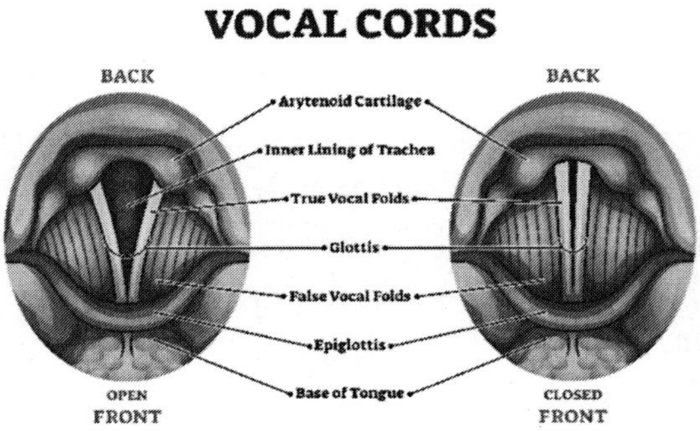

VOCAL CORDS

Figure 5: The larynx viewed from above (transverse plane)

Various muscles are attached to the cartilages of the larynx, including the thyroarytenoid, lateral and posterior cricoarytenoid, cricothyroid, and oblique and transverse arytenoid muscles. Some anatomists and healthcare professionals identify the upper part of the thyroarytenoid muscle as a distinct muscle, referring to it as the vocalis muscle.

The synchronous contraction and relaxation of these muscles move the cartilages, altering the length and tension of the vocal folds, which modifies pitch during phonation.

The hyoid bone is horseshoe-shaped and is classified as a floating bone, meaning it is not directly attached to any other bones. However, muscles of the tongue and larynx are attached to this bone. Because the tongue muscles are connected to the hyoid bone, excessive retraction of the tongue can pull the hyoid bone downward. This can dampen vocal resonance, reduce the efficiency of vibration, and lead to muscle tension in the larynx.

During inhalation, the posterior cricoarytenoid muscles abduct the vocal folds, moving them away from the midline of the glottis and widening the vocal aperture, which allows air to enter the lungs.

For phonation and singing, the lateral cricoarytenoid muscles adduct the vocal folds, bringing them together at the midline. The transverse and oblique arytenoid muscles also contribute to this adduction. As airflow is directed through the vocal folds, they vibrate, creating sound.

During vibration, subglottic air pressure builds beneath the vocal folds, forcing them apart from the bottom to the top. Once they separate, the airflow is released, and the vocal folds are sucked back together from bottom to top, initiating a wave-like movement. This phenomenon is known as the Bernoulli effect, and it plays a key role in the production of sound during phonation.

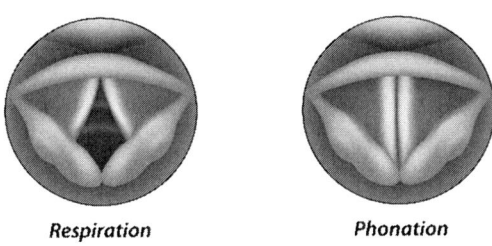

Respiration *Phonation*

Figure 6: Vocal folds position during respiration and phonation

To produce a lower pitch, the vocal folds must relax and loosen. This occurs when the thyroarytenoid and vocalis muscles pull the vocal folds forward, towards the thyroid cartilage. However, the thyroid cartilage itself remains mostly stationary.

For a higher pitch, the vocal folds need to stretch and tighten. This is achieved by tilting the thyroid cartilage and contracting the cricothyroid muscles, which elongate and tense the vocal folds. Consequently, looser vocal folds create a lower pitch, while tighter, more elongated folds produce a higher pitch.

In singing, the vibrating column of air is intentionally shaped and manipulated by the tongue, teeth, jaw, and lips. The spaces in the chest, throat, mouth, and nose also modify and shape the sound produced by the vocal folds.

Together, the manipulation of these structures generates a unique resonance, sound quality, and expression. These structures are referred to as resonating chambers. The individual differences in the shapes created by these resonators contribute to a voice that is distinct to each person. It is essential to embrace, appreciate, and celebrate our own unique voice.

The Pharynx

The pharynx is a muscular tube connected to the larynx that serves as a pathway for air, sound (voice), and food during swallowing. It is located behind the nasal and oral cavities, as well as the larynx. The pharynx is divided into three sections: the nasopharynx, oropharynx, and laryngopharynx (also called the hypopharynx) (Figure 7).

Anatomy (Larynx / Pharynx)

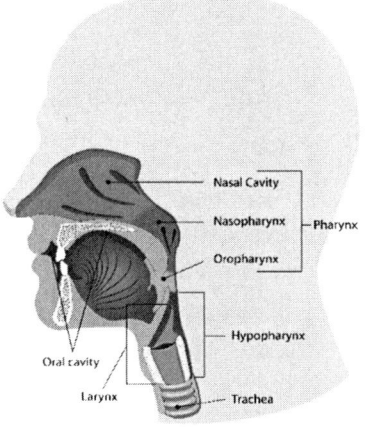

Figure 7: The Pharynx

The size and shape of the pharynx can be modified by the pharyngeal muscles to amplify the voice and modify sound frequencies. One common modification is called the "open throat" technique, where the pharyngeal space is kept open and relaxed. This relaxed, open pharynx also promotes smoother airflow, which is essential for maintaining steady, controlled vocal production, especially during sustained notes.

When the pharynx is narrowed by the contraction of these muscles, a different vocal quality is produced. This manipulation of the pharyngeal muscles can create both bright and dark vocal tones.

The Nasal Cavity

Located in the nose, the nasal cavity extends from the nostrils to the back of the throat. The nasal cavity is narrow and is made up of mucous membranes and irregularly shaped bones. It can be separated from the oropharyngeal cavity by raising the soft palate, which seals off the two cavities.

Although the nasal cavity cannot be modified during singing because it is composed of bones and cartilage, it naturally plays a role in the resonance of certain sound frequencies. It enhances specific harmonics of the voice, helping to balance the quality and clarity of the voice. This ensures the tone is neither overly nasal nor excessively guttural.

Nasalized consonants and vowels are found in languages such as French and are also used in contemporary commercial singing for vocal effect.

The Oral cavity

The oral cavity plays a crucial role in singing. By altering its shape and size through movements of the jaw, lips, tongue, and soft palate, singers can amplify sound, enhance clarity and articulation, and enrich vocal resonance.

Jaw

The jaw, also known as the mandible, articulates with the temporal bone at the temporomandibular joint (TMJ), allowing for jaw movement. While it may seem that opening the jaw wider produces a louder sound, the jaw's movement is primarily a hinging action, facilitated by the TMJ. When the jaw opens too widely, it moves forward from its resting position, which can reduce resonance, distort sound, increase muscle tension, and make it more difficult to sustain notes and phrases. Achieving the right balance in jaw movement is crucial for optimal vocal production.

Lips

Appropriate lip shaping and positioning in singing help to reduce tension, produce clear and resonant vowels, facilitate enunciation, and achieve the desired vocal timbres. Over-articulation, excessive lip puckering, tightening, licking, or biting can create unnecessary tension, dampen sound, dry out the lips, and interfere with smooth vocal production and airflow. Additionally, inconsistent lip shaping can compromise clarity and consistency in vocal quality and sound.

Tongue

The resting tongue is typically positioned close to the roof of the mouth, with the root of the tongue attaching to the inside of the mandible, and the back of the tongue connecting to the hyoid bone.

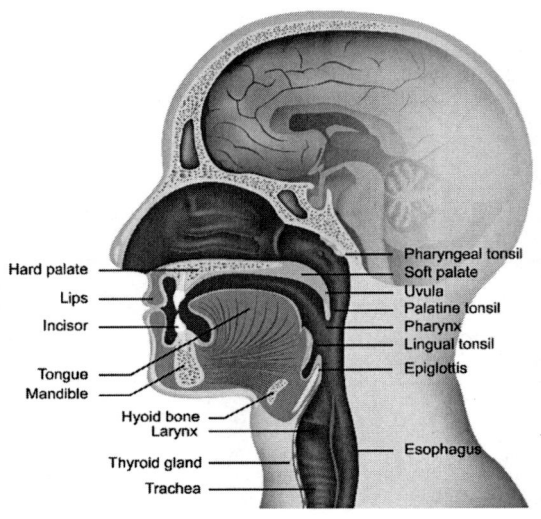

Figure 8: Diagram – The tongue

The tongue's position is crucial for producing vowels and consonants in singing. It is manipulated more actively in singing, as its position significantly influences the quality and clarity of the sound produced.

If the tongue is positioned too low and pulled back during singing, it can dull the sound, hinder articulation, cause pitch instability, and contribute to tension in the laryngeal muscles, negatively affecting vocal performance. Conversely, if the tongue is positioned too high, it can increase nasality, restrict resonance, and lead to pitch instability, muscle tension, and articulation difficulties.

Therefore, maintaining a relaxed, neutral tongue position is essential for optimal vocal technique. This balanced approach helps achieve a clear, resonant sound with minimal tension and maximum control.

The Hard and Soft Palate

The hard palate, located at the front of the roof of the mouth, plays a key role in articulating sounds, especially those where the tongue presses against it, such as in the production of "t" and "d" sounds. Additionally, it reflects sound waves, contributing to the enhancement of vocal resonance.

At the back of the roof of the mouth lies the soft palate (velum), which can be raised or lowered to control the opening of the nasal passages. When raised, the soft palate blocks airflow through the nose, which is essential for producing non-nasal sounds. The position of the soft palate also significantly impacts the resonance and quality of the tone produced. For example, raising the soft palate enlarges the resonating space within the oral cavity, boosting specific frequencies and enriching resonance, resulting in a brighter, more vibrant tone. Conversely, when the soft palate is lowered, it allows airflow through the nasal cavity, producing a darker, mellower tone.

Although singing demands precise coordination of numerous muscles and structures, it also relies on a complex network of brain regions working together to orchestrate these muscle groups.

Singing And the Brain

Numerous cortical and subcortical brain regions are activated during singing. Cortical areas such as the primary motor cortex, premotor cortex, somatosensory cortex, auditory cortex, prefrontal cortex, and temporal lobes work together in a coordinated manner to support various aspects of singing, including motor control, sensory feedback processing, auditory perception, and cognitive functions (e.g., memory, emotional regulation). While cortical areas are crucial for singing, subcortical structures also play an important role. These subcortical structures include the basal ganglia, thalamus, cerebellum, and brainstem. Subcortical areas work in conjunction with cortical regions to ensure the smooth execution of vocal activity, as well as the mapping and recall of specific musical elements.

Achieving success as a singer involves understanding the anatomy and physiology of singing, recognizing the strengths and weaknesses in our voice, and working to improve technique. By addressing potential voice issues and disorders (e.g., dysphonia) and developing efficient vocal techniques, singers can manage vocal pressures, tasks, and demands. This ultimately leads to greater confidence in using the voice effectively and safely over extended periods.

Vocal Health

Vocal health is crucial for singers, as the voice is subject to numerous pressures and demands. It serves not only as a musical instrument and a means of communication but, for professional singers, also as a source of income. Prioritising vocal health enables singers to maintain vocal quality and longevity while reducing the risk of injury.

Emotional states, both positive and negative can influence vocal and physical responses. For example, when a negative event occurs, the body may enter a fight or flight response. The brain processes this information, and the body often reacts by altering posture, heart rate, and breathing patterns, while also creating muscular tension. These physiological changes can affect how the voice mechanism functions and alter vocal quality.

During these stressful situations, the voice may sound strained, and singers may experience tension and tightness in the muscles. Pitch and volume may be affected, and speech may become rapid and less clear due to the increased rate. Prolonged stress can result in ongoing tension and strain on the vocal apparatus, potentially leading to soreness, hoarseness, vocal loss, pitch breaks, and vocal fatigue.

Therefore, maintaining vocal health, both physically and emotionally, is essential for singers to ensure a high-quality, sustainable voice. A natural voice is balanced and clear; it is flexible and suited to the individual's needs. As singers, it is important to become familiar with our own voices and understand how to use them in a safe and natural way.

Effective voice production depends on:

- A good breath supply that is easily controlled from the centre of the body.
- A relaxed body and proper posture, free from tension that may interrupt airflow or constrict the throat.
- A healthy larynx, including well-functioning muscles and cartilages of the throat
- The ability to imagine an easy flow of sound through an open throat and jaw.
- Proper sound placement, focusing the resonance toward the front of the mouth and face rather than holding it back or pushing from the throat.

Dysphonia

Singers use their vocal apparatus extensively. As a result, they are at greater risk of developing dysphonia. Dysphonia is a broad term that refers to a voice disorder characterized by an atypical voice quality that does not meet the functional or communicative needs of the individual. It can be classified as either structural or functional.

Structural dysphonia arises from physical changes to the vocal folds or surrounding structures. These changes can often be identified through visual examination, such as laryngoscopy. Structural abnormalities include vocal nodules, vocal polyps, laryngitis, vocal fold paralysis, Reinke's oedema, and laryngeal cancer. Such lesions may result from vocal abuse (e.g., shouting, prolonged strain, or overuse), poor vocal hygiene, infection, smoking, nerve damage, or laryngeal trauma.

Functional dysphonia occurs when no physical or structural abnormalities are present, yet the voice still sounds impaired. It is often associated with vocal misuse, psychological factors, or muscle tension. Reflux, particularly laryngopharyngeal reflux (LPR), is also classified as functional dysphonia because it originates from acid reflux. However, if left untreated, LPR can cause tissue damage in the larynx, potentially resulting in structural dysphonia.

For singers, dysphonia may affect their singing voice, impacting performance ability. They might notice changes in vocal range, pitch, tone, tonal control, vocal quality, the ability to clearly sustain notes, and reduced vocal strength and endurance. In severe cases, singers may lose the ability to sing altogether. Dysphonia can also affect the speaking voice, often presenting as a rough, breathy voice with reduced volume, vocal strength, and pitch control, including pitch breaks.

If vocal changes or issues persist, whether in singing or speaking, it is crucial to seek early guidance from a qualified voice professional, such as an ENT specialist or a speech-language therapist. Delayed intervention can turn minor concerns into more serious conditions. The following section will help singers identify and understand common vocal issues to prevent long-term damage. However, professional guidance is strongly recommended as a first step.

Vocal Fatigue

Vocal fatigue refers to vocal tiredness and is commonly caused by overuse, improper technique, inadequate breath support, and dehydration. It can result in a reduced vocal range and difficulty sustaining notes.

To manage vocal fatigue:

- Incorporate vocal rest into your singing routine, especially after intense use.
- Ensure adequate hydration
- Use proper vocal and breathing techniques.
- Warm up and cool down the voice appropriately
- Avoid vocal abuse, such as shouting or speaking loudly for prolonged periods.
- Avoid singing in uncomfortable or painful vocal ranges.

Laryngitis

Laryngitis is an inflammation of the larynx, which often results in hoarseness or loss of voice. It can be short -term (acute) or long-lasting (chronic) and it affects the vocal folds, impairing normal voice production.

Laryngitis can be caused by viral infections, acid reflux, voice overuse, vocal strain, and allergies. Symptoms typically include a rough and breathy voice, sore throat, and a dry cough.

In the event of Laryngitis:

- Rest the voice until all symptoms resolve.
- Maintain adequate hydration.
- Avoid whispering, and speak only when necessary. Use alternative forms of communication, such as text-to-speech or writing, if needed.
- Avoid irritants and pollutants, such as smoke.
- Consider using a humidifier to keep the throat moist and support healing.

Reflux

Reflux is a condition whereby stomach acid flows back into areas it shouldn't, potentially affecting the oesophagus, throat, and vocal folds. There are two main types relevant to vocal health:

• Gastroesophageal Reflux Disease (GERD): This occurs when stomach acid travels up into the oesophagus. Common symptoms include heartburn, chest discomfort, and regurgitation of food or liquids.

• Laryngopharyngeal Reflux (LPR): This occurs when stomach acid travels even higher, reaching the throat and larynx. Unlike GERD, LPR can present without heartburn. Instead, it may cause throat irritation and voice changes.

LPR is particularly concerning for singers and voice users, as it can irritate the vocal folds and larynx, leading to inflammation and vocal strain.

Common symptoms of LPR include:

- Frequent throat clearing
- A persistent burning sensation or the feeling of a lump in the throat (globus sensation)
- A rough or breathy voice
- Vocal fatigue and reduced vocal control
- Chronic cough or a dry throat

Dehydration

Dehydration occurs when the body does not receive enough water. This can result from insufficient water intake or excessive consumption of dehydrating substances such as caffeine, sugary drinks, or alcohol. When dehydrated, the throat can become dry, and thick mucus may build up, which can interfere with vocal function and lead to vocal fatigue.

In the events of dehydration:

- Drink water consistently throughout the day. Don't wait until you feel thirsty or attempt to compensate by drinking large amounts at once.
- Avoid caffeinated, sugary, and alcoholic beverages, as they can contribute to dehydration.

Throat Tension

Throat tension can result from improper vocal and breathing technique, as well as psychological and physical stress, particularly tension in the head, neck, and shoulders.

This may lead to symptoms such as tightness or strain around the throat, reduced vocal projection, and vocal fatigue.

In the event of throat tension:

- Engage in physical and psychological relaxation techniques (e.g., stretching, breathing exercises, mindfulness).
- Focus on appropriate voice use, breathing, posture, and body alignment exercises to reduce tension.
- Work with a singing teacher or voice coach to improve technique and minimize strain during singing.

Some Do's and Don'ts

Do:

- Warm up your voice properly before use
- Rest your voice as much as possible, especially when it feels tired
- Take time to breathe properly
- Drink plenty of water throughout the day
- Take regular breaks during practice or performance
- Use steam inhalation as needed to help lubricate and relax the throat

Don't:

- Don't shout or force your voice. This includes talking over background noise.
- Don't clear your throat excessively, and try to avoid coughing. Instead, sip water, swallow firmly, or yawn to relieve the urge.
- Don't smoke or expose yourself to smoky environments.

Top Tips for a healthy voice

- ***Hydration***

Drink plenty of water throughout the day to keep the vocal folds hydrated. Aim for at least 8 glasses of water daily; however, more may be needed depending on your activity levels and environmental conditions. For example, dry environments may require increased fluid intake.

Be mindful of dehydrating beverages, such as alcohol, caffeine, and sugary drinks, and aim to limit or avoid these.

- ***Carry out Warm Up and Cool Down Exercises***

Always warm up your voice, body, and mind before singing with gentle exercises.

Cool down the voice, body, and mind after singing to help reset to a natural state.

- ***Avoid Vocal Strain***

Avoid shouting, screaming, or speaking loudly for extended periods.

Use appropriate vocal techniques and proper support to prevent strain when singing high or powerful notes.

Avoid over-projection in loud environments. Consider using voice amplification (e.g., a microphone) to reduce strain.

- ***Practice Good Mind, Body and Vocal Technique***

Work with a registered Vocal Coach or Singing Teacher

Work with a vocal coach or singing teacher to ensure correct vocal and body techniques.

Be mindful of your emotions and manage stress levels accordingly.

Avoid pushing or forcing the voice, especially when singing outside your comfortable pitch range.

Avoid whispering, as it can strain the voice.

- ***Manage Reflux and Diet***

Acid reflux can damage the vocal folds. Avoid spicy, acidic, or fatty foods, especially before singing.

Do not eat large, heavy meals before singing, and avoid lying down immediately after eating. Remain upright for at least 45 minutes after a meal to aid digestion.

- ***Allow Vocal Rest***

Particularly after intensive use, incorporate periods of vocal rest into your routine.

Ensure you get adequate sleep to help the body and voice heal.

If vocal rest is necessary, consider communicating the main idea only, and explore other means of communication, such as writing, pictures, text, or text-to-speech apps. Maintain a natural voice whenever possible.

- ***Avoid Smoking and Pollutants***

Avoid smoking, passive smoking, and exposure to pollutants, as these can irritate the throat and damage the vocal folds.

Toxins, such as chemicals, dust, and dry air, may irritate the throat and damage the vocal folds.

Use a humidifier if possible.

- ***Maintain a healthy lifestyle***

Regular exercise and a well-balanced diet contribute to optimal vocal health. Washing your hands frequently and avoiding illness also support vocal well-being.

If you are sick, do not push your body or voice; prioritize rest. Listen to your body and be mindful of vocal fatigue, pain, or any changes in voice and vocal quality.

If persistent vocal changes occur, book a consultation with a voice specialist or an ENT (Ear, Nose, and Throat) professional.

In the event of a sore throat:

- Drink plenty of water.
- Increase your intake of multivitamins and minerals by eating fruits and vegetables or using supplements.
- Prioritize physical and vocal rest
- Steam inhalation (using hot water) can help rehydrate the vocal folds and clear nasal congestion. (Avoid adding oils to the water, as these can have a drying effect.)

- If you lose your voice or experience pain, avoid singing and minimize speaking. If the problem persists, seek medical advice.

How to Practice Effectively

Why practice?

While the role of the teacher is important in supporting, providing necessary information, tools, and encouragement to guide the student's learning, each student must ultimately take ownership of their own journey.

Part of the learning process, therefore, involves developing an understanding of independent practice. When individuals recognize practice and independent learning as integral components of their experience as musicians, they are more likely to have a positive and fulfilling experience with their tuition.

The images below demonstrate the relationship between practice and motivation for students. Regular practice boosts confidence, leads to improvement, and elicits positive feedback, which, in turn, enhances motivation and self-esteem. In contrast, when a student does not practice, their progress is inevitably affected, leading to a loss of confidence and motivation.

Positive practice cycle Negative practice cycle

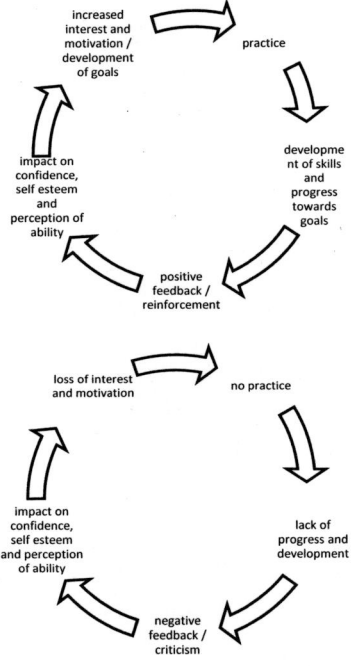

The Practice Cycle

For singing students, this can be a challenging area, as many feel self-conscious and uncomfortable practicing in spaces where they might be overheard. Additionally, it can be difficult to practice singing when the individual requires support to scaffold the melody line. Fortunately, most students have access to mobile phones, which makes it possible to record breathing and vocal exercises that can be accessed independently, along with vocal lines and piano accompaniments for any repertoire. In more contemporary styles, students can also find backing tracks online.

Ideally, students should practice regularly, using the time to become familiar with their voice and explore the strategies and techniques covered in lessons. All practice should include a variety of warm-up activities to prepare the voice and reinforce technical aspects of singing. The following list outlines a range of activities that can be adapted to create a warm-up session.

Warm up

Before engaging in intense singing, it is crucial for singers to warm up their voices, much like athletes warm up before a big game or intense physical activity. For safe, efficient, and effective singing, warm-up exercises are important for several reasons:

- Warm-up exercises gradually prepare the vocal folds, torso, chest, diaphragm, and body by increasing blood flow, making them more responsive and flexible. This helps prevent strain or injury and increases stamina.
- Warm-ups gently stretch the vocal folds, allowing singers to reach both high and low notes with ease and control. This process improves vocal range.
- Warming up helps achieve a clearer, richer, and more consistent tone. It smooths out any roughness, providing singers with a more polished and controlled sound.

- Many warm-up routines include breathing exercises, which are crucial for increasing breath control. This is essential for sustaining long phrases and singing with power, without straining the voice.
- Warming up also prepares singers mentally by enabling them to focus on their voices, the sensations experienced in the body, the notes, music, and techniques. It's an excellent way to manage nerves and get into the right mindset for singing.
- A good warm-up can help prevent vocal fatigue, allowing singers to sing for longer durations.
- Warm-up activities don't only focus on vocal sound and breathing exercises. Warming up the body before singing is equally important and makes a significant difference in vocal production. It helps relax and release tension, particularly in the neck, shoulders, and jaw—areas that often carry stress. When these muscles are relaxed, the voice can flow more freely without feeling tight or strained.
- Good posture is another important aspect. By warming up the body, the back, shoulders, and core muscles can be loosened, aiding alignment and ultimately improving breath control and vocal projection.

In this section, warm up and cool down activities are broken down into mental, body, posture, breathing and vocal exercises.

Mental Exercises

These mental warm-up techniques can boost focus, confidence and overall performance in singing, making singing sessions more productive and enjoyable.

Visualisation

Picture your performance or practice: Close your eyes and imagine yourself performing confidently. Think about how you look, how you sound, and how audiences, teachers, and others are reacting. What positive comments are they giving you? This mental visualization can boost your confidence and help you mentally prepare for a performance or class.

Environment

Find a space where you feel comfortable, confident, and positive when singing.

Breathing Exercises

Although specific breathing exercises are used for singing, they can also be incorporated into your mental preparation routine. However, it is important to note that deep breathing for mental preparation differs from diaphragmatic breathing, which is necessary for singing. Therefore, singing-specific breathwork exercises will still be required after completing this mental exercise.

Deep Breathing

Find a comfortable spot to sit or stand, then take slow, deep breaths. Breathe in through your nose for a count of four, hold for four, and exhale through your mouth for six. This helps calm your mind and prepare your body for singing. Be mindful that deep breathing is distinct from diaphragmatic breathing.

Positive Affirmations

Repeat encouraging statements such as, "I'm a highly talented, competent, and confident singer," or "I'm ready to give my best today." These positive affirmations can lift your mood and reduce any nervousness.

Mindfulness Meditation

Spend a few minutes focusing on your breath and being present in the moment. If your mind starts to wander, gently bring it back to your breathing. This can help reduce stress and improve focus. As with deep breathing exercises, mindfulness practice breaths are different from the breaths required for singing.

Mental Rehearsal

Visualize yourself singing through the songs you'll be working on. Picture how you'll deliver the lyrics and hit the notes. This can help you feel more prepared and less anxious.

Attention Exercises

Choose a simple task, such as focusing on a specific sound or object for a few minutes. This can help improve your concentration during singing practice.

Journaling

Spend a few minutes jotting down your goals for the session, performance, or any concerns you may have. Reflect on how these concerns have arisen, what is within your control, and what is beyond your control. This practice helps clear your mind and set a clear intention for your practice. Afterward, it is beneficial to reflect on these notes to assess the accuracy of any earlier statements or concerns you addressed before singing.

Gratitude Practice

Take a moment to think about or write down things you are thankful for, including aspects of your singing journey. This can help you stay positive and open-minded.

Setting Intentions

Think about what you want to achieve in a class or performance, whether it's mastering a specific skill or simply enjoying the process. Setting clear intentions can help guide your focus and motivation.

Body Exercises

Side Neck Stretch

Gently tilt your head to one side, bringing your ear toward your shoulder without raising the shoulder. Hold for 10–15 seconds, then switch to the other side.

Neck Rolls

Slowly roll your head in a circular motion, first clockwise, then counterclockwise. Keep the movement gentle and avoid overstretching.

Shoulder Rolls

Forward and Backward Rolls:
Roll your shoulders forward in a circular motion for 10–15 seconds, then reverse and roll them backward. You can also vary this exercise by making one shoulder move forward and the other backward for five repetitions, then switch.

Face

Jaw Massage

Gently massage the muscles around your jaw and cheeks with two fingertips in a circular motion. Open and close your mouth slowly while massaging to release tension in the jaw.

Jaw Stretches

Gently open your mouth and hold for five seconds, then release.

Move your jaw side to side in a relaxed manner five times on each side.

Chewing

Start by pretending you're chewing something chewy. Make large, exaggerated movements with your lips and jaw, letting your mouth open wide as you "chew." Do this silently for about 30 seconds. Then, continue the same exaggerated movements, but this time, add your voice. You may find yourself yawning, which is a sign of relaxation. Try humming or making soft vocal sounds while you "chew."

Yawn – sigh

Start by gently placing your tongue against your lower teeth. Then, open your mouth wide, like you're making a big yawn. Keep your soft palate raised, your tongue low, and stretch out the back of your throat. As you do this, let out a soft sigh of breath as quietly as possible. You might even trigger a real yawn, which is perfectly fine and a good thing! Repeat this stretch about five times.

Tongue Stretches

Stick your tongue out as far as possible and hold for a few seconds, then relax. Repeat by stretching your tongue in different directions (up, down, left, right). This helps reduce tension in the tongue and improves articulation.

Body

Side body stretch

Raise one arm overhead and gently lean to the opposite side, stretching the side of your body. Hold for 10–15 seconds, then switch sides.

Hip Flexor Stretch

Step one foot forward into a lunge position, keeping the back leg straight and the heel lifted. Gently press your hips forward to stretch the hip flexors. Hold for 15–20 seconds, then switch legs.

Movement

March on the spot for 1 minute to increase blood flow in the body.

Do remember that everything is connected. The purpose of the breathing and technical exercises is to develop the skills that allow you to sing your chosen repertoire effectively. Be conscious of your posture, breath, and voice placement, and avoid switching off this awareness when you begin singing a piece of repertoire.

The diaphragm is another muscle vital to singing. Therefore, it also needs to be warmed up to help with vocal efficiency and quality, and to reduce strain and injury.

Diaphragmatic Breathing Warm-Up Exercise

- Get into a comfortable position, such as lying on your back with your knees bent and feet flat on the floor. Alternatively, sit comfortably in a chair with a straight back.
- Place one hand on your chest and the other just below your ribcage (on your belly) to help feel the diaphragm movement.
- Inhale slowly through your nose, allowing your belly to rise as your diaphragm expands, keeping your chest relatively still. The focus should be on the belly expanding rather than the chest.
- Exhale gently through your mouth, letting your belly fall. You can purse your lips slightly to aid breath control. The focus should be on the belly moving, and the chest should remain mostly still. Repeat a few times.
- Towards the end of this warm-up, you can progress to exhaling with "f", "sss", and "sh" sounds, followed by "vvvvv", "zzzz", and "ʒ" (as in "su" in meaSUre or treaSUre) a few times. This will provide significant abdominal movement and help expel excess or unwanted air. You can extend the duration of the exhale for more control.
- Continue to focus on relaxing your body and releasing any physical and psychological tension.

Vocal warm up exercises

Semi-occluded vocal tract exercises (SOVTE)

Semi-occluded vocal tract (SOVT) exercises have been used for many years, particularly in training singers and other vocal performers. They are part of a longstanding tradition that helps individuals find their optimal vocal technique. For example, tube phonation has been documented as existing prior to the twentieth century. This approach was developed more recently by Dr. Marketta Sihvo, a Finnish speech and language therapist, and Dr. Ilter Denizoglu, a Turkish otolarypngologist, who proposed the Lax Vox method (Sihvo & Denizoglu, 2007; Denizoglu, I. and Sihvo, M., 2010). However, Dr. Ingo Titze's research into the biomechanical and acoustic properties of the vocal folds and vocal tract led to the formal development, categorisation, and expansion of SOVTE (Titze, 2006). He discovered that partially occluding the vocal tract (such as through straw phonation) created favourable conditions for vocal fold vibration, optimising airflow and pressure relationships.

SOVT exercises offer four key benefits for singers:

- They work by creating back pressure that balances the air pressure above and below the vocal folds. This balance enables the vocal folds to vibrate more efficiently and with less effort, reducing strain and the risk of vocal injury. The back pressure also provides valuable feedback, improving sensory awareness of

optimal vocal fold position and efficiency, making it easier to fine-tune vocal techniques.
- SOVT exercises naturally encourage the lowering of the larynx while reducing tension in the surrounding muscles, promoting a more relaxed singing posture. These exercises also enable the vocal folds to adduct more gently, protecting them from the wear and tear that can occur with intense singing.
- They enhance the interaction between the vocal folds and the resonating spaces in the vocal tract, creating a fuller and more resonant sound without additional effort.
- SOVT exercises partially close off the vocal tract. This partial closure encourages steady and controlled airflow, which improves breath management and dynamic control, such as volume regulation.

Common SOVTE exercises

Rigid Straw Phonation

Using one hand, place a rigid straw (approximately 9 cm in length and 2 to 3 mm in diameter) between your lips, ensuring a firm yet comfortable seal. For children, use a shorter straw. Maintain proper posture and neck alignment throughout the exercise.

Begin by producing a neutral, sustained vowel sound (do not focus on a specific pitch or tone) for one minute, either as a warm-up or cool-down. Inhale through the nose as needed. If no sensation is felt in the mouth and throat, gradually increase the loudness to increase back pressure. Ensure there is no bulging of the cheeks or leakage of air from the lips or nose.

If any tension, discomfort, or pain is experienced, reduce the loudness to alleviate pressure. Over time, progress this exercise to about 3 minutes. To further engage the vocal range, try singing scales or a simple song through the straw.

Blowing through a Resonance Tube (Lax Vox technique), (Sihvo & Denizoglu, 2007; Denizoglu, I. and Sihvo, M., 2010).

The Lax Vox technique is a form of semi-occluded vocal tract exercise that involves blowing air through a resonance tube (straw) while phonating. This method helps balance airflow and pressure in the vocal tract, reducing strain on the vocal folds and promoting more efficient vocal fold vibration.

For this exercise, a silicone tube measuring 35 cm in length and 9–12 mm in inner diameter, along with one-third of a container (such as a glass or bottle) filled with water, are recommended.

Find a comfortable, upright position with good posture. Sit or stand with your back straight and shoulders relaxed. Begin with diaphragmatic breathing: inhale deeply through your nose, allowing your abdomen to expand, and exhale slowly through your mouth. This will help engage your breath support.

Using one hand to hold the straw and the other on the container, place the straw between your lips, ensuring a relaxed but secure fit. Gently blow air through the straw, creating a consistent, steady stream of bubbles. Next, produce and sustain a neutral vowel sound gently through the straw, starting with 1 minute and progressing to 3 minutes.

Progress to gliding up and down your vocal range while phonating through the straw. You can then progress to simple scales and short melodies. Always ensure correct posture and neck alignment, maintain relaxed and consistent airflow, and avoid pushing or straining your voice. Pay attention to how your voice and vocal apparatus feel. The goal is to produce a sound that is smooth, even, and free of strain. You should feel the vibrations in your lips and possibly in your face.

Lip Trills

Relax your lips and blow air through them to create a bubbling sound, similar to that of a motorboat. Start with simple sustained pitches or gentle glides from low to high and back down. Progress to singing scales or short phrases while maintaining the trill.

Tongue Trills

Roll your tongue (like a rolled / Spanish "R" sound) while producing sound. Begin with gentle, sustained notes, then try gliding through your vocal range or singing scales.

Humming

Close your lips and hum lightly, focusing on producing a relaxed and resonant sound. Vibrations should be felt on your lips, which may cause a light tickling sensation. Start with sustained notes at a comfortable pitch, then glide gently up and down your range. You can also hum scales or simple melodies.

Cheek puff

Gently close your lips without creating a tight seal around them. Puff out your cheeks evenly by filling them with air. Try to maintain even expansion and avoid letting air escape through the corners of your mouth. Begin phonating softly at a comfortable pitch, making a gentle sound while maintaining smooth airflow.

Traditional vocal warm up exercises

Sirens/ NG Sound (as in the end of the word "sing").
Start on a comfortable pitch, sustaining the sound. Glide up and down your vocal range, keeping the sound light and relaxed.

Gentle Scales and Arpeggios

Sing simple scales or arpeggios on a comfortable vowel (such as "ee") at a moderate tempo, starting in the middle of your range and gradually expanding higher and lower.

Tips for vocal warm up exercises

- **Maintain good posture and alignment**.
- **Engage in diaphragmatic breathing and controlled airflow**, focusing on proper breathing

techniques, pay attention to where the breath is located.
- **Work on controlling the inhale and exhale**, noting where the breath is located, and focus on softening the core to breathe from the lower abdomen.
- Start slowly and increase complexity and demand gradually.
- **Monitor your mental and physical sensations** to avoid unnecessary tension.
- **Avoid mental and physical tension** during exercises.
- **Warm up the entire body** to support vocal performance.
- **Warm up the entire vocal range**, gradually addressing both higher and lower registers.
- **Look in a mirror if possible** to ensure proper body alignment and posture, this helps "activate" the body.
- **Sirens and lip trills** typically help to awaken the voice.
- **Maintain a relaxed** state throughout the warm-up.
- **Mentally prepare** by thinking through what you plan to work on in the session.
- **Use triads and arpeggios** across a range of vowels and consonants to connect the breath to the voice.
- **Engage in specific exercises** to improve tone, flexibility, and intervallic movement, as needed.
- **Focus on specific sections** of the repertoire, such as runs, intervals, and extended passages, addressing aspects like balance, articulation, character, or dynamics.

These activities can then be followed by work on selected repertoire. However, students should aim to work on specific aspects of each piece, such as balance, articulation, character, or dynamics, rather than simply singing through each song. This approach helps develop an understanding of the various components involved.

Cool down

After intense or prolonged singing sessions and performances, the mind, body, and vocal folds can become fatigued. Performing cool-down exercises is just as important as warm-up activities for several reasons: to promote recovery, prevent injury, and improve overall performance. For example:

- **Cool-down exercises help to gradually reduce vocal effort**, preventing the vocal folds from experiencing abrupt relaxation that could lead to strain or damage.
- **They help maintain flexibility and prevent stiffness** in the vocal folds and surrounding muscles.
- **Vocal fatigue** can occur when the voice is pushed too hard without proper care, which is especially important for singers who perform frequently or for long durations.
- **Gentle cool-down exercises promote blood circulation** to the vocal folds and surrounding muscles. Increased blood flow aids the healing process, especially if there has been minor strain or swelling.

- **Singing often involves controlled breathing techniques**. Cool-down activities can help restore natural breathing patterns, allowing the body to relax and return to its normal state.
- **Cool-down exercises provide a mental transition** from specific activities, such as rehearsal or performance mode, to rest. This transition helps singers relax and reflect on their performance in a calm, supportive manner.

Cool down exercises

Mental

Reflection

- Reflect on two positive aspects of the session and one area for improvement, setting a SMART goal (Specific, Measurable, Achievable, Realistic, Time-bound). For example, two positives could include: "*I sustained a note without experiencing discomfort.*" The area for improvement might be: "*I was uncertain of the notes and timings in the middle section.*" The SMART goal could be: "*By the end of the week, I will be more confident in the notes and timings in the middle section of X song by practicing this section for 15 minutes each day.*"
- Record any emotions encountered during the session or performance, and reflect on the reasons behind these emotional responses.

- Establish a relaxing post-singing routine, such as making a cup of tea, listening to music, or reading a book, to signal the end of the singing session.
- Engage in self-care rituals that promote relaxation and recovery
- Practice mindfulness to aid in mental and physical recovery after the session

Body exercises

- Base of Tongue

The base of the tongue is located just above the throat, extending toward the back of the mouth. It can be accessed externally from the underside of your chin, just behind the jawline.

Begin by gently rubbing or tapping under the chin with your fingertips. Next, place your thumb or index finger under the chin, just behind the jawline. The rest of your fingers may rest comfortably in a fist position. Gently press upward with the thumb or index finger into the soft tissue under the chin. A slight firmness where the base of your tongue rests may be felt, accompanied by some discomfort due to tension.

If specific areas of tension are present, hold gentle pressure on those points for 10-15 seconds. This technique, known as trigger point release, helps relax the muscle fibres at the base of the tongue.

Gently massaging the base of the tongue area in small circular motions can also be performed, as well as a back-and-forth motion. Gradually increase pressure as tolerated, but always ensure comfort. Focus on areas that feel tight or tender, but avoid pressing too hard to prevent discomfort.

After this massage, gently stretch the tongue by extending it as far as is comfortable and moving it side to side. This helps release any lingering tension.

This technique can be very effective in reducing tension in the tongue and throat, thus supporting better vocal performance and overall vocal health.

- Neck massage

Place your left hand on the left side of your neck. Your thumb should face the front, and your fingers should face the back. Massage in a circular motion from the base of the skull to the bottom of the neck. Repeat a couple of times, then swap hands and sides.

- Jaw massage

Gently massage the muscles around your jaw and cheeks with two fingertips in a circular motion. Open and close your mouth slowly while massaging to release tension in the jaw.

- Jaw stretches

Gently open your mouth and hold for five seconds, then release. Move your jaw side to side in a relaxed manner five times on each side.

Breathing

- Deep breathing and gradually reducing breath volume: Gradually decrease the depth, duration, and intensity of your breaths, allowing your breathing to become quieter and more natural. This progressive reduction helps your body ease back into a resting state.
- Gentle sighs can further promote resting breathing patterns. Take a deep breath in and exhale with a soft, relaxed sigh.

Upper Back and Shoulder Stretches

- **Cross-Body Shoulder Stretch**
- Bring one arm across your body and use the opposite arm to gently pull it toward you. Hold for 15–30 seconds, then switch arms.

Upper Back Stretch

- Clasp your hands together and reach them forward, rounding your upper back. Hold for 15–30 seconds.

Progressive Muscle Relaxation

- Tense and Relax
- Focus on tensing each muscle group, then relaxing it, starting from your toes and working up to your head. This technique helps identify and release any remaining tension.

Vocal exercises

- Gradually reduce the intensity and duration of Semi-Occluded Vocal Tract exercises, such as gentle humming, light lip trills, and straw phonation. These exercises help balance the pressure above and below the vocal folds, optimizing vocal fold vibration and reducing vocal fold collision forces. This supports vocal recovery and reduces strain.
- The yawn-sigh technique promotes relaxation of the vocal tract and reduces tension in the throat and larynx. It also encourages the lowering of the larynx and opens the pharynx, which can help alleviate tightness caused by singing.
- Vocal rest (no talking) – Allow your voice to rest after vocal use.

Top Tips for Cool Down

The goal of a cool down is to help reset the mind, voice, and body to their natural state, gradually leading toward relaxation.

- Avoid hyperventilating during the cool down. If you feel out of breath, stay calm, take deep, gentle breaths, pause, close your eyes, and spend a few moments focusing on calming your mind and breathing.
- Incorporate resting-state breathing techniques after every singing session to help train your body to return to normal breathing more easily over time.

- Perform all exercises gently, with gradual reductions, and avoid pushing into positions that cause discomfort.
- Pay attention to how your body and voice feel, and adjust the exercises as needed.
- Always wash your hands thoroughly before performing any massage.
- Apply gentle pressure and avoid causing discomfort or bruising during massages and stretches.
- If you experience pain or significant discomfort, stop the massage and consult a licensed practitioner, such as a voice specialist, for guidance.
- Reflect on any learning or reflective points to improve your practice.

Getting Ready For a Performance

For many singers, performing can be a real highlight, but exams, assessments, and public performances can also be stressful, regardless of age or ability, and require careful planning and preparation.

Performing from memory

While some singers may find it difficult to memorize repertoire, this should be the goal, as performing from memory allows the individual to focus entirely on the physical act of singing and convey the character and meaning of the piece more effectively.

On the day

Before any performance, including practical grade exams, singers should ensure they warm up properly. This can either take place before the performance in a suitable space, or individuals may prefer to warm up in shorter bursts throughout the day, taking 10 to 15 minutes at regular intervals to focus on breathing and run through some scales and arpeggios. However, it is important not to over-sing before a performance, no matter how tempting this might be. Singers should avoid lengthy rehearsals or long practice sessions immediately before a performance or exam.

Performance anxiety

It is normal for everyone to experience some level of nerves before performances and exams. This is a natural human response to a stressful situation. The degree of performance anxiety can vary based on several factors, including the age, personality, experience, and confidence of the singer, as well as the nature, significance, and context of the event and the level of preparation beforehand. The key thing to remember before any performance is to prepare effectively, as this will alleviate much of the anxiety related to presentation and delivery.

Useful strategies for managing performance anxiety include breathing exercises, meditation, and positive visualization before the event itself. As you wait to begin, try to mentally rehearse the performance, imagining everything going perfectly. Remember, the audience (including adjudicators and examiners) is on your side and wants you to succeed.

Part 2
Practical Exercises for Singers

The next section of this book presents a range of practical exercises for singers, with strategies to help develop and enhance effective posture and breath control, along with a set of useful vocal exercises.

Posture

'Feet – Hips – Heart – Head'

Posture is a vital element in effective voice production and is closely related to breathing. The central core must be strong and secure in order to provide sufficient space to inhale properly and allow the body to fully "support" the sound. With this in mind, the following sequence can help in establishing good posture for singing and vocal projection.

Feet: The feet should be slightly apart and facing forward. Aim to adopt an active stance with the weight balanced towards the front of the foot rather than the heels. Try to grip into the floor with the toes—think of holding yourself down.

Knees: If you are able, bend the knees slightly and make sure that you are not locking the joint—stay flexible.

Hips: Start by gently moving the hips from side to side and forward and back until you find a comfortable place in the centre. Consider the space between the hips—imagine a line across the lower abdomen and lift this line without moving anything else. This is the base of your triangle.

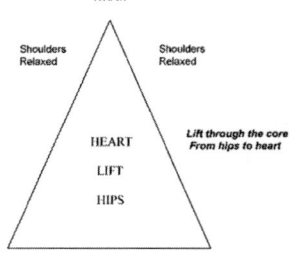

Heart: Now consider lines from your hips to your heart forming the sides of your triangle and then stretch up through the triangle. Keep the shoulders down (try imagining you have heavy elbows) and the rest of the body relaxed.

Head: Imagine a piece of string pulling you up through the top of your head. Keep the shoulders relaxed and the chin level at a 90 degree angle to the floor.

Breathe: Inhale and exhale for a few minutes and focus on the following:

- Where do you feel the inhale? Is it in the shoulders? Try to open up the rib cage, relax the tummy and inhale more slowly to allow the breath to travel lower into the lungs.
- What happens as you exhale? Do you feel your abdomen collapsing? Try to focus on lifting the air out from the core. Keeping the shoulders down and relaxed, lift through the core to the very end of the breath.

Breathing Exercises

"Inhale and Exhale"

Inhale:

- Breathe out, emptying your lungs of air.
- With an open, relaxed mouth (not overly wide) take a slow, silent breath in for 4 counts.
- Make sure you are not moving your shoulders and/or upper body (it may help to imagine you have heavy elbows) and keep the stomach muscles relaxed. Try to feel the breath in the lower rib cage, focusing on the side and back of the ribs.

Exhale on "Shh or Tss":

- Inhale and exhale on "shh" or "tss" for 8 slow counts.
- Be aware of the breath behind the teeth to the very end
- Maintain control and focus on a steady stream of air.
- If this is quite easy, try getting louder throughout

- Do Not Deflate.
- As you approach the end of the breath, you will feel a tightening across the lower abdomen – the line between the hips will appear to move in and up – this is normal. Keep going and keep lifting through the core.
- Once you are happy controlling the exhale for 8 counts, move on to exhale for 12, 16, 20 and 24 counts (breathing in for 4 slow counts beforehand each time).
- Keep the shoulders down and lift through the core throughout. The key feature of this exercise is control. Explore how the end of the breath really feels – we generally inhale long before we have reached the end of the breath.
- When you reach the end of the breath drop the jaw and take a natural breath in without moving the upper body.

Inhale and staccato "ch":

- Inhaling for 4 counts as above (shoulders are down and the breath is slow and silent), you should now replace the exhale breath with a series of short, sharp, hard "ch" sounds. (Imagine the word chip).
- Do not breathe between the "ch" sounds.
- You should initially aim for 16 in one breath, getting louder as you go along. The sounds should be short and explosive with no voice.

- You should feel the abdomen moving as the diaphragm supports the sound.
- Once you are comfortable with 16, aim for 24 and then 30 – all in one breath with no inhale between sounds.

Extension to staccato "ch" exercise:

Now try the same exercise using 'ts' (the end of the word bits).

This exercise helps to connect the diaphragm with the consonants and can lead to a more supported vocal production.

Note – the shoulders should be still throughout and the posture strong – think "feet – hips – heart – head".

Paper on wall exercise:

- You will need a piece of paper approximately 7cm x 7cm.
- Stand facing a wall – it must be a flat, even surface.
- Take one step backwards (still facing the wall), place the piece of paper on the wall at the same height as your mouth and hold the two outer edges using your fingertips.
- Lean forward, inhale slowly and start to produce a consistent stream of air focused on the centre of the piece of paper.
- Now take your hands away and hold the piece of paper in position using only your breath for a count of 8. This will involve a consistent flow of air. DO inhale slowly and silently before attempting the exercise and maintain a strong core throughout.

Vocal Exercises

Lifting the Soft Palate

To achieve a relaxed open position and ensure the soft palate is lifted, try the following exercise:

- Inhale, then, on any note sing on an 'ng' sound (imagine the end of the word 'sing') for 4 beats. Then open up onto an 'ah' for 4 beats. This will effectively lift the soft palate and relax the throat.
- If you find particular phrases, notes or exercises tricky and feel a tightening in the throat, try starting then on an 'ng' and opening up once you have established the sound.
- Consider the internal shape of the mouth at all times.
- Simply opening the lips as wide as possible can be counterproductive. Imagine a small new potato, piping hot in your mouth and this will help to recreate the sensation of creating a central space. This can help in finding a relaxed mouth shape.

Notes on breathing and pitch

One common problem for singers involves tension when moving from the lower register into the upper register during the same phrase. One useful strategy to help with this is to consider the highest note in the phrase before you begin. Breathe as if you are about to sing this note and aim to keep the whole phrase lifted to the approximate pitch of this note. In pieces where the range is tricky, try breathing and placing the notes as if they are an octave higher. It may also help to visualise phrases as straight lines. Rather than *'up and down'*, think *'out and in'*.

Tongue Position

The tongue is actually a ball of muscle with its root in the throat. The main advice for singers is to maintain a relaxed and largely inactive tongue in order to avoid tension, which impacts the larynx. This is easier on some consonants than others and it is worth spending some time enunciating each specific consonant in order to feel the movement of the tongue for each. Pay attention to consonants that involve the tongue directly, including "n", "l", "y", "s", "j", "k", "z" and check that you are not anticipating the action related to these in your singing. When in doubt, practice in a mirror and watch the action of the tongue and try the soft palate exercise to help find a natural space and tongue position in the mouth.

Jaw Tension

Issues relating to tongue tension are also often linked to problems with the jaw. The most important thing to remember is to keep a relaxed, natural, "floppy" jaw at all times. Try any of the exercises in this book on a loose "yah, yah, yah" and try to really let go of any gripping or tension, as this will translate into the sound and can also lead to discomfort.

Vowel Exercise

Try saying the following quite normally: A E I O U.
Apart from "E", each involves a series of sounds which, when sung are unhelpful to the line and resonance. To help create pure vowel sounds, try the following:

- Instead of A, sing "ah".
- Instead of I, sing "ee".
- Instead of O, sing "or".
- Instead of U, sing "oo".

Now, practice singing these pure vowel sounds and replacing English vowels with "pure" vowel sounds in your singing – whatever the language.

Articulation

Singing in any language involves a distortion of the original sounds of the words. This is because when we sing any tune, we extend through the vowels, as this is where the voice carries the melody and this extension changes the sound of the vowel. It is worth taking time to say the words of any song in slow motion in order to identify where the vowel is being stretched and how to shape it. Above all, remember…we don't sing in the same way that we speak.

Watch your Diphthongs!

A diphthong is a sound formed by the combination of two vowels in a single syllable, in which the sound begins as one vowel and moves towards another. These are particularly tricky when singing in English and words such as "day," "loud," "die," and "down" can cause problems for singers as they involve traveling through differing vowel sounds on one note.

When approaching diphthongs, remember that in most cases, you need to extend and travel along the first of the vowel sounds concerned. It can be very useful to say the word in slow motion to work out the pure vowel sounds involved. So, in the word "sigh," for example (slow motion sah-ee), extend the "ah" for as long as possible before resolving onto the "ee" at the end of the note.

Examples of diphthongs and vowel pronunciations:

Day, May, Say	air –	ee
Die, My, Cry, Sigh, Lie, High	ah –	ee
Loud, How, Proud, Crowd	ah –	oo
Down, frown, crown, Round, Found	ah –	oo

'A selection of singing exercises for use in developing projection, breath control and even tone.'

1. Even Tone

- Start by inhaling slowly and quietly through an open mouth. Then try exercise 1a, singing through this simple scale exercise to gently warm up. Aim for a relaxed, easy tone on "shore", "shoe" or "shah", starting with a strong "sh". Think of the highest note as you inhale and sing in a straight line, thinking out and in rather than up and down.

Exercise 1a

- Next, try the following triad pattern. Sing each note on a short "ha", as if laughing. You should feel this in the abdomen; if not, make the "h" stronger. Aim to sing this (as if laughing) until you reach the end of the breath.
- Then try exercise 1b, starting on different notes across the vocal range, singing the same pattern smoothly and in one breath on any of the following extended vowel sounds. Use the consonant at the beginning to help project onto the vowel and make

sure you maintain the tone through to the very end of the breath.

- **"shore", "wore", "pore", "yore", "far", "jar", "shah", "shee", "wee", "fee"**

Exercises 1b

2. Arpeggio exercise

This exercise has various extension activities that can increase the level of difficulty for more experienced students. The aim is to achieve an even tone across the vocal range.

- Begin exercise 2a by inhaling slowly and quietly through an open mouth (thinking of the highest note in the exercise) and singing on an open 'ah' or 'or' in one breath, aiming for an even tone across the range. To increase the challenge, alternate legato and staccato, then increase the number of arpeggios so that you sing up to 7 or 8 in one breath.

Exercise 2a.

- In addition, start lower in the voice and gradually move up, starting the exercise on higher notes each time. You can choose to sing all legato, all staccato or alternating staccato and legato.
- This exercise is useful for improving breath control and projection and for promoting an even tone.

Extended arpeggio exercise

- Exercise 2b introduces an extended arpeggio and is a little more challenging as the pattern is longer and includes more movement. Again, this exercise can be

sung legato or staccato and on most vowel sounds. Perhaps consider starting on a "sh", "v" or "z" to help project onto the vowel.
- Sing the exercise at a moderate speed to begin with and try slowing it down to really focus on tone and challenge breath control.

Exercise 2b.

* Consider singing the exercise through twice or even three times in one breath, maintaining a consistent tone throughout.

3. Descending thirds with short breath

This begins higher in the vocal range and is useful since many students fall flat while descending. In addition, at the end of bar 2, there is a breath after the dotted crotchet G, which provides an excellent opportunity to practice taking a big breath in a smaller space. Keep the shoulders down, relax the stomach muscles and open the mouth to inhale.

✓ = short breath - drop the lower jaw.

- Start by breathing in slowly and quietly through an open mouth, lifting up to the pitch of the first note and staying there throughout the exercise on an open "ah" or alternating "ee" and "ah".
- As you descend, avoid deflating or sinking vocally. When you reach the dotted crotchet in the middle, keep the mouth open as you breathe in so that it is a natural progression from the note – treat the breath as part of the music rather than a pause.
- Lift throughout – especially towards the bottom and avoid the urge to sink into the final note.

4. Intervals

This is an excellent exercise for ironing out bumps between the head and chest voice and helping produce an even tone.

If practiced staccato, this exercise can help to develop the connection with the diaphragm, thereby strengthening tone and improving projection.

- As with Exercise 2, there are a range of extension activities to make this even more enjoyable. Start by inhaling slowly and quietly through an open mouth at the pitch of the highest note.
- It is vitally important that you concentrate on the higher note throughout, crescendo through the repeated higher note if possible as this will increase the focus. Start the exercise in various places across the vocal range.
- Avoid bumping or changing gear as the intervals get wider and try to keep the notes even in tone. Singing on an "or" or an "ah", aim for 2 slow legato arpeggios in one breath and then try some staccato repetitions, aiming for three very bouncy staccato runs in one breath.
- To make the staccatos more effective (and to make sure the shoulders aren't doing all the work) stretch the arms out throughout.

5. Ascending and descending thirds

This is an effective exercise for those who are anxious about moving into the upper register.

- Start by breathing in slowly and quietly through an open mouth. Think of the highest note in the exercise and sing on an "ah"; think out and then in on the descent rather than up and down.
- To help in creating a more even tone, start with the palms together in front of the face. During the ascending part of the exercise, gradually stretch the arms out so that by the breath in the middle the arms are fully outstretched. In the second half of the exercise, the hands should return to the starting position. Stay very still throughout and focus entirely on the hands.
- The breath in the middle should be a natural extension to the preceding note – keep the mouth open on an "ah" and try to stay relaxed through the core and lower ribs as you inhale.

6. Introduction to Staccato

The style of staccato singing here is very specific.
- Start by saying the word "hot" 4 times, exaggerating the 'H'.
- Next, sing the word 'hot' 4 times on any note, exaggerating the "h". The quality of tone is not important; rather, the connection with the diaphragm is the focus in this exercise.
- Start by breathing in slowly and quietly through an open mouth, thinking of the pitch of the highest note (the staccato note) in the exercise. Do start this exercise in various places across the vocal range.
- Singing on an "ah", the first three notes should be legato followed by three very staccato notes (exaggerated "h" on the beginning of each one if necessary). The final 4 notes are legato.

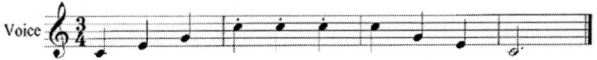

7. Extended Staccato arpeggios

This provides an opportunity to further develop the staccato singing, which in turn will help strengthen the tone and projection by encouraging a greater connection between voice production and the diaphragm.

- After breathing in slowly and quietly through an open mouth, thinking of the upper note, these should be sung with a great emphasis on the beginning of the sound – the most effective sound for the purpose is the word "hot" without the "t" at the end.
- Aim for 3 arpeggios in one breath, making sure that each one is connecting with the diaphragm. Start the exercise in various places across the vocal range.
- As with exercise 4, to prevent the shoulders from doing all the work and to feel this really working, stretch the arms out wide with palms forward throughout.

8. Skipping

This exercise incorporates both legato and staccato as the phrasing requires the singer to lift off the quaver, making them staccato without breathing.

- The whole exercise should be sung in one breath. Start by breathing in slowly and quietly through an open mouth to the pitch of the highest note and sing on "ah".
- Lift off on every quaver and allow the semiquavers to run smoothly. Try this exercise starting on different notes.
- If possible, sing through twice in one breath avoiding the temptation to descend at the end of the first run as this will make the second more difficult.
- To free the voice and increase the fun, stretch the arms out and swing them around the body (aim for full rotation of the upper body) whilst singing.

9. More Extended arpeggios

This is an exercise in three parts.

- First learn the initial arpeggio pattern to "ah".
- Breathe in slowly and quietly through an open mouth to the pitch of the highest note and be sure to stay lifted throughout – avoid descending and focus on singing out and in rather than up and down.
- Once the initial pattern is comfortable, repeat three times, first time f, second time p, third time super staccato.
- Aim to start the exercise on different notes to fully warm up the vocal range.

10. Hysterical Owl

This exercise is wonderful for really exploring the connection between the voice and the diaphragm.

- Start by breathing in slowly and quietly through an open mouth, then place one hand on the abdomen and one hand with the palm in front of the mouth.
- The five – note pattern is to be sung super staccato to "hoo, hoo, hoo, hoo, hoo" with an exaggerated 'H'.
- This should be followed each time by a short breath with a dropped jaw.
- The connection on the breath should be evident throughout.

11. Ways into running

The legato required for this exercise resembles exercises 1 and 2. When practicing this exercise, start by singing through each phrase separately, then put the first two together and then try all three in one breath. The whole exercise should be sung in one breath on any vowel other than "ee".

- Breathe in slowly and quietly through an open mouth to the pitch of the highest note.
- Aim for a still line and simply think through the notes rather than singing every single one too deliberately.
- As with the other exercises, focus on "out and in" rather than "up and down".

The next exercise includes words – aim to exaggerate every consonant and extend fully through each vowel – no skipping or scampering! The four staccato notes at the end are an optional extra and must be sung in the same breath as the preceding run.

- Aim for a controlled line throughout and try starting on various notes.

References

Sihvo, M. and Denizoglu, I., 2007. Lax vox voice therapy technique. *PEVOC, Groningen, The Netherlands.*

Denizoglu, I. and Sihvo, M., 2010. LaxVox: voice therapy technique. *Curr Pr ORL*, *6*(2), pp.284-95.

Titze, I. R., (2006). Voice Training and Therapy with a Semi-Occluded Vocal Tract: Rationale and Scientific Underpinnings. *Journal of Speech, Language, and Hearing Research*, *49*(2), pp.448-459.